What Would You Do?

THE REVOLUTIONARY WAR BEGINS

Would You Join the Fight?

Elaine Landau

Enslow Elementary

an imprint of

Enslow Publishers, Inc.

40 Industrial Road
Box 398
Berkeley Heights, NJ 07922
USA

http://www.enslow.com

Enslow Elementary, an imprint of Enslow Publishers, Inc.

Enslow Elementary® is a registered trademark of Enslow Publishers, Inc.

Library of Congress Cataloging-in-Publication Data

Landau, Elaine.
   The Revolutionary War begins : would you join the fight? / Elaine Landau.
      p. cm. — (What would you do?)
   Includes index.
   Summary: "Explores the beginning of the Revolutionary War, discussing the causes and leaders of the
rebellion, and how the first shots fired at Lexington and Concord began America's long road to
independence"—Provided by publisher.
      ISBN-13: 978-0-7660-2900-2
      ISBN-10: 0-7660-2900-X
      1. United States—History—Revolution, 1775–1783—Causes—Juvenile literature. 2. United States—
History—Revolution, 1775–1783—Biography—Juvenile literature. I. Title.
      E210.L36 2008
      973.3'11—dc22

                                                      2007041836

Printed in the United States of America

10 9 8 7 6 5 4 3 2

To Our Readers:
We have done our best to make sure all Internet Addresses in this book were active and appropriate when
we went to press. However, the author and the publisher have no control over and assume no liability for
the material available on those Internet sites or on other Web sites they may link to. Any comments or
suggestions can be sent by e-mail to comments@enslow.com or to the address on the back cover.

♻ Enslow Publishers, Inc., is committed to printing our books on recycled paper. The paper in every book
contains 10% to 30% post-consumer waste (PCW). The cover board on the outside of each book contains
100% PCW. Our goal is to do our part to help young people and the environment too!

CONTENTS

Britain sent soldiers to the colonies in 1768 to enforce the Stamp Act and the taxes that came with it.

ANGRY
ABOUT TAXES

Think back to an earlier time. Imagine you are in the American colonies in the 1760s. There are many problems. You can see that people are not happy.

Britain ruled over the colonies. Yet the colonists enjoyed a lot of freedom. They chose their own officials and settled their own **disputes**.

George III of England was their king. However, it had been years since the first colonists arrived.

King George III began to change the laws for the colonies.

Paul Revere made this picture of the port of Boston. Boston was one of the cities to which tea was shipped.

An American colonist used this stamp. Colonists were required to buy the stamp for certain items. Many colonists felt that this law was unfair.

By now, many colonists had been born in America. Not everyone felt as close to Britain as the early colonists did.

Most colonists liked things as they were. However, in the 1760s, King George III and the British government, called **Parliament**, began to make some changes. Britain needed money and started taxing the colonies.

In 1765, the British passed the Stamp Act. They now required a government stamp on many items, like newspapers and playing cards. The colonists had to pay for the stamps. This type of payment was called a tax.

Later, in 1773, the British placed a tax on tea. Tea was a popular drink. So this tax could be costly.

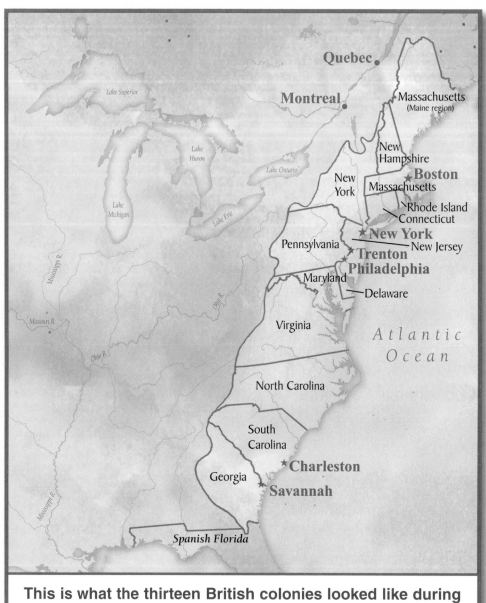

This is what the thirteen British colonies looked like during the 1770s.

The colonists were angry about the taxes. They felt that the British government did little for them. They did not think they should be taxed.

WHAT WOULD YOU DO?

What if you were King George III? *Would you . . .*

* **Deal gently with the colonists? You do not want them to rebel. Perhaps they will agree to lower taxes.**

* **Do away with the taxes completely? You could look for the money elsewhere. The colonists might fight you if you keep the taxes. A war would cost a lot of money, and many people could be killed.**

* **Be firm with the colonists? You are the king and they are your subjects. Show them who is in charge.**

KING GEORGE STANDS FIRM

King George III did not give in. After all, he was the king of England. He wanted both the colonists' respect and their tax dollars.

Some colonists still refused to pay the unfair taxes. Now they united to fight back. They formed a number of **patriot** groups.

One of the most active groups was the Sons of Liberty. Two important leaders had helped form it. They were John Hancock and Sam Adams.

King George III and the British government saw these men as troublemakers. They wanted Adams and Hancock out of the picture.

Sam Adams was a member of the Sons of Liberty.

10

Members of the patriot group the Sons of Liberty often met at the Green Dragon Tavern.

They hoped they would catch the pair. Then these rebels would be hanged.

Many colonists saw things differently. To them, Hancock and Adams were heroes. The colonists knew that they had to protect them.

WHAT WOULD YOU DO?

What if you were John Hancock? You were once a wealthy and respected merchant. Now you are a wanted man. *Would you . . .*

* Continue on this rebellious path? If you are arrested by the British, you could lose everything. You might even be hanged! Would you dare to lead the colonists against the king?

John Hancock

HANCOCK CONTINUES TO REBEL

Both John Hancock and Sam Adams were not about to back down. They found ways to rebel against British taxes. On December 16, 1773, the colonists protested the tax on tea. They tossed 342 chests of British tea into Boston Harbor.

Today we know this event as the Boston Tea Party. The colonists

This is one of the actual tea chests from the Boston Tea Party. Only two are known to still exist today.

People on Griffin's Wharf watched and cheered as colonists rowed off to toss the tea into Boston Harbor.

had tea parties in other harbors too. These actions made King George III very angry.

The king and Parliament sent soldiers to Massachusetts and the other colonies. They came to keep order. New laws were also passed limiting the colonists' freedoms.

Because of the Quartering Act, British soldiers could order colonists from their homes. The colonists were also ordered to supply food to the troops.

The colonists could no longer elect their own officials. The British government picked them instead. Public meetings were not allowed either.

The Quartering Act was passed in 1774. Under this law, British soldiers could live anywhere their officers chose. This included the colonists' homes.

SOLDIERS FOLLOW ORDERS

The British soldiers simply followed orders. Most did not care how the colonists felt anyway. Their loyalty was to the British king and to Parliament.

General Thomas Gage was in charge in Massachusetts. On April 14, 1775, he received some special orders from Britain. He and his soldiers were to arrest John Hancock and Sam Adams. The pair was hiding out in Lexington.

General Gage was the leader of the British soldiers in the colony of Massachusetts.

In the 1770s, American colonists made this musket.

The British soldiers then were to go on to Concord. The colonists had hidden weapons there. General Gage wanted those weapons destroyed.

The raid would take place on April 18. The British hoped to surprise the colonists. If successful, they could hurt the rebel's cause.

WHAT WOULD YOU DO?

What if you were Margaret Kemble Gage? She was General Gage's wife, who was born in the colonies. You overheard your husband discussing the attack. You do not want to betray him. Yet you do not want the king to crush the colonists. *Would you . . .*

* **Alert the rebels? What do you think Margaret Kemble Gage did?**

COLONISTS LEARN OF THE RAID

Luckily, the colonists learned of the raid. We may never know if General Gage's wife, Margaret Kemble Gage, told anyone about the raid. Dr. Joseph Warren was a close friend of Mrs. Gage. He knew of the attack ahead of time. Some people think she told him.

Dr. Joseph Warren was a patriot. He warned other patriots and called on two people to help.

Dr. Joseph Warren found out about the British raid before it occurred.

Paul Revere made things out of silver. He made a punch bowl (at bottom) in 1768. The painting is by John Singleton Copley.

One of the people was **silversmith** Paul Revere, who was also in the Sons of Liberty.

On the evening of April 18, Warren asked Paul Revere to ride to Lexington. He was asked to warn Hancock and Adams that the British were coming. After that, he was to ride on to Concord to warn the colonists there.

Colonists had formed their very own fighting groups called **militias**. In Massachusetts, these

Minutemen often made their own weapons.

men were known as **minutemen**. They were proud that they could be ready to fight in a minute's notice. Now they would be put to the test.

Revere had been a messenger for the patriots before. Tonight he would have to ride as fast as he could to get to Lexington and Concord before the British.

WHAT WOULD YOU DO?

What if you were Paul Revere? *Would you . . .*

✳ **Agree to do this? The British will be on the lookout for rebels tonight. If you are caught, you could be arrested or even hanged! Would you be willing to take the risk?**

REVERE TRIES TO WARN THE COLONISTS

Paul Revere agreed to go. He also asked a friend to help with this dangerous task. His friend was to use lanterns to let the colonists know the British troops' route to Lexington.

One lantern in the Old North Church steeple meant that the British were going by land. Two lanterns meant that they were crossing the Charles River by boat. This way, if Revere were

Paul Revere would wait for a signal from the Old North Church.

William Dawes, Jr., a patriot, also rode to Lexington.

caught, the patriots would still know how the British were coming.

Revere took the same route as the British that night. He first crossed the Charles River by boat. When Paul Revere reached Charlestown, the patriots had a fast horse waiting for him.

Dr. Warren had sent another messenger out that night. It was a thirty-year-old patriot named William Dawes, Jr. Dawes took the land route the whole way to Lexington instead of crossing the Charles River. Warren had wanted the two messengers to take different routes. If the British caught one, the other might still get through.

At first, things went well for Revere. Then two British soldiers spotted him. They thought he might be a rebel messenger and went after him.

At the left, Paul Revere starts off on his historic ride. Revere and Dawes took different routes. They both hoped to avoid British patrols. Another rider, Samuel Prescott, later joined them.

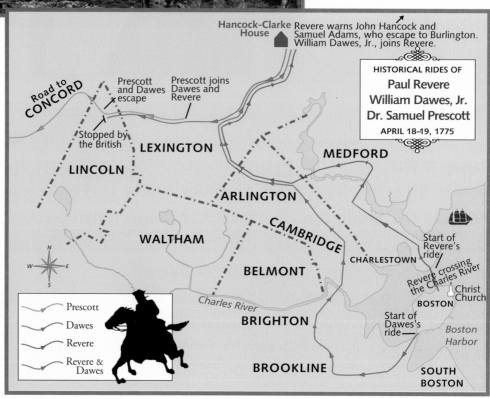

Hancock-Clarke House

Revere warns John Hancock and Samuel Adams, who escape to Burlington. William Dawes, Jr., joins Revere.

Road to CONCORD

Prescott and Dawes escape

Prescott joins Dawes and Revere

Stopped by the British

LEXINGTON

LINCOLN

MEDFORD

ARLINGTON

CAMBRIDGE

WALTHAM

CHARLESTOWN

BELMONT

Start of Revere's ride

Revere crossing the Charles River

Christ Church

BOSTON

Charles River

BRIGHTON

Start of Dawes's ride

Boston Harbor

BROOKLINE

SOUTH BOSTON

HISTORICAL RIDES OF
Paul Revere
William Dawes, Jr.
Dr. Samuel Prescott
APRIL 18–19, 1775

N W E S

Prescott
Dawes
Revere
Revere & Dawes

WHAT WOULD YOU DO?

What if you were Paul Revere?

Would you . . .

* Try to outrun the British? If you give up now, you will have failed in your mission.

* Surrender to the soldiers? If you try to run, you might be shot. You would be of no use to the rebel colonists if you were dead.

* Try to outsmart the soldiers? You could make them think that you are a silversmith and nothing more. Then maybe you can still get to Lexington before the British.

Paul Revere's house in Boston is a historic site that can be visited today.

REVERE GETS AWAY

Revere decided to make a run for it. Before long, the British soldiers were left far behind. As Revere rode

on, he passed farms and houses. He called out to warn the colonists that the British were on their way. This let those in the militia get ready for the attack.

By midnight, Revere had reached the house where Hancock and Adams were hiding. Both Revere and Dawes got there before the British.

Paul Revere got away from the British soldiers.

However, Revere never made it to Concord that night. He was stopped by British soldiers on the way. Though they did not arrest him, they took Revere's horse. That way he could not warn the Concord colonists.

WHAT WOULD YOU DO?

Hancock and Adams realized they had enough time to escape. *Would you . . .*

* **Leave if you were one of them? You know that the British are on their way. There is likely to be fighting.**

* **As a true patriot, should you stay and fight with the minutemen? The other patriots want you to leave. They do not want you to risk death or arrest.**

Should you stay, or should you go? What do you think is the right thing to do?

HANCOCK AND ADAMS ESCAPE

Both Hancock and Adams left before the British arrived. If they had stayed, they could have been captured or killed. The patriots needed these valued leaders alive.

Before long, 77 minutemen had gathered at Lexington. Both young and old men came to face the British. They were led by Captain John Parker, whose own grandfather was under his command.

The minutemen did not have to wait long for the enemy. Very early that morning, about 250 redcoats arrived at

The minutemen in Lexington got ready for the British soldiers. Here, an actor is dressed like a minuteman.

John Parker led the minutemen of Lexington. This statue was made in honor of him.

Lexington. British soldiers were called **redcoats** because of the red jackets of their uniforms. British Major John Pitcairn led them. These soldiers were well-armed, well-trained, and ready for action.

A larger **force** of 450 British soldiers was led by Lieutenant Colonel Francis Smith. It was not far behind the first group of redcoats.

The 77 minutemen rushed to the Lexington village green. Pitcairn rode up to the men and told them to put down their **firearms** and go home. Captain Parker saw that his men were badly outnumbered. He did not want them needlessly killed. He told the men to leave but to keep their firearms.

Both sides had been told not to shoot. Yet suddenly a shot rang out from somewhere. The British were sure it came from the rebels. They began firing into the group.

The battle of Lexington was quick. But it was also deadly for the colonists.

The minutemen fired back. The shooting only lasted about ten minutes. When it was over, eight minutemen were dead. Ten more had been **wounded**.

None of the British had been killed and only two were wounded. It had been a quick and easy victory for them. While the dead minutemen were still on the green, the

A colonial soldier wore a three-cornered hat called a tricorn hat. The hat at the right dates back to the American Revolution.

British soldiers even cheered. The colonists were shocked and angry.

Now most of the British soldiers wanted to go back to Boston. They felt no need to go on to Concord. They believed that they had taught the rebels a lesson that day.

A group of British soldiers spoke with Lieutenant Colonel Smith and asked him to lead them home.

WHAT WOULD YOU DO?

Colonel Smith knew his men were tired. Yet he felt that the job was only half done. What if you were Colonel Smith? *Would you . . .*

✳ **Go on to Concord?**

✳ **Head back to Boston?**

THE BRITISH GO TO CONCORD

Colonel Francis Smith led some 700 British soldiers to Concord. The colonists at Concord were ready for them. They had buried or hidden most of their weapons and supplies. Word of what happened at Lexington had already spread. So minutemen from nearby towns began arriving at Concord to help.

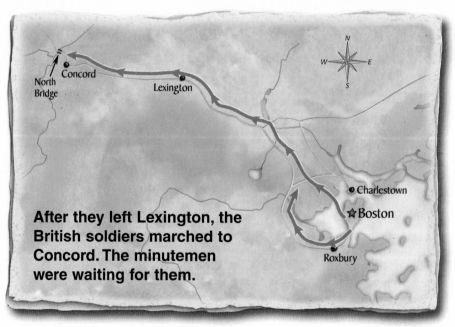

After they left Lexington, the British soldiers marched to Concord. The minutemen were waiting for them.

Minutemen said goodbye to their families as they prepared for the battle in Concord.

Before long, about 250 minutemen had gathered. Sixty-five-year-old Colonel James Barrett was in charge of the force. Barrett saw that he now had a good number of men. However, the group was still no match for 700 trained British soldiers.

A minister blesses a minuteman as he leaves to fight in Concord.

WHAT WOULD YOU DO?

Colonel Barrett had some important choices to make. If you were Barrett, *would you . . .*

* **Fight the British there in the heart of Concord? Not all the weapons and supplies were moved in time. Maybe you can stop the British from burning and looting the town.**

* **Attack the British a bit farther out at North Bridge? Fewer British soldiers are posted there. Strike these men first. Then it will be easier to take on the others.**

* **Send all the men home? There is no sense in fighting when you are outnumbered. Supplies and weapons are not worth as much as a man's life.**

MINUTEMEN FIGHT BRAVELY AT NORTH BRIDGE

Barrett decided to attack the British at North Bridge. The minutemen had not put up much of a fight at Lexington. So the British expected another easy victory at North Bridge.

But, the British were in for a big surprise. Even more minutemen arrived from other towns. Soon Barrett had from three to four hundred men.

These minutemen fought with all their

The colonists battled the British redcoats at the North Bridge in Concord.

The attack by the colonial soldiers soon became too much for the British.

might. There were men killed on both sides. Many were wounded.

Now, the British grew fearful. They watched as more minutemen kept arriving. They were not sure they could defeat the growing colonial force.

WHAT WOULD YOU DO?

What if you were British officer Colonel Francis Smith? You see that it might be hard to beat these minutemen. *Would you . . .*

　＊ **Stay and finish the fight?**

　＊ **Retreat and head back to Boston?**

COLONEL SMITH HEADS BACK TO BOSTON

Colonel Francis Smith chose to retreat. He saw no point in fighting on. The British had already destroyed as much of the rebels' **stockpile** as they could find.

Smith did not want to lose any more men. He took some wagons from Concord to put his wounded men in. Then he headed for Boston.

The British soldiers retreated from Concord back to Boston.

This statue in Minuteman National Historical Park honors the brave fighting men at Lexington and Concord.

By now, quite a few militia leaders were at Concord. They had some difficult choices to make as well.

WHAT WOULD YOU DO?

If you were a militia leader, *would you . . .*

* Just be happy that the British gave up and sent their men home?

* Plant minutemen at different points on the route back to Boston? They could shoot at the redcoats as they marched by.

THE MILITIAS KEEP FIGHTING

The militia leaders decided that the fight was not over. They posted their men along the route to Boston. They turned the road into a long battlefield. Some shot at the British from houses and barns. Others hit their targets from behind trees, bushes, and stone walls.

The colonial soldiers shot at the redcoats the whole way back to Boston.

The names of the men who were killed at Lexington and Concord were listed on a piece of paper called a handbill, so colonists could see if loved ones had died.

The British were not used to fighting this way. They usually faced their enemy on an open battlefield. Now they had to fight men they could not see.

The British soldiers' pride in their Lexington victory quickly faded. At this point, they only cared about **dodging** rebel bullets. By the time they reached Boston, 73 British soldiers had been killed and 174 more were wounded. The colonists had beaten the best-trained army in the world!

The minutemen had losses too. Yet one thing was clear—they had won that day! The fighting at both Lexington and

The British surrendered to the Americans at Yorktown, Virginia, in 1783. By then, the United States had declared its independence. It had become a country itself!

Concord proved to be the first battles of the American Revolution.

They marked the start of a long, hard struggle for the colonists. The war with Britain did not end until eight years later in September 1783. By then, the colonists had finally earned their independence. The thirteen colonies became the United States of America. A country's birth began with the shots fired at Lexington and Concord.

TIMELINE

1760s—King George III of England begins heavily taxing the colonists.

1765—The Stamp Act is passed.

1773—A new tax is placed on tea.
December 16: Colonists protest the tax by throwing 342 chests of tea into Boston Harbor. This comes to be known as the Boston Tea Party. Soon afterwards the King sends British troops to the colonies.

1774—*June 2:* The Quartering Act is passed.

1775—*April 14:* General Thomas Gage receives special orders from Britain to plan a raid.
April 18: Gage's raid begins. Paul Revere and William Dawes, Jr., ride to warn other colonists.
April 19: Early in the morning, the British soldiers arrive at Lexington. The British win a quick and easy victory over the minutemen. Later in the day, the British lose at Concord. The minutemen also attack the British soldiers on the road back to Boston. The fighting at Lexington and Concord mark the start of the American Revolution.

1783—*September:* The colonists' eight-year war with Britain ends. The thirteen colonies have won their independence.

WORDS TO KNOW

dispute—A disagreement between people or nations.

dodging—Avoiding something by moving away quickly.

firearms—Various types of guns.

force—A unit or group of trained soldiers.

looting—The taking of goods from an enemy during war; also, any form of stealing.

militia—A group of soldiers trained to fight in emergencies.

minutemen—Massachusetts soldiers during the American Revolution who were ready to fight in a minute.

Parliament—The ruling government in Britain; Parliament members pass the nation's laws.

patriot—The name of colonists fighting against the British.

rebel—To fight against; also, a person involved in a fight against a government.

redcoat—A British soldier.

retreat—To go back or leave a battle.

silversmith—Someone who makes items out of silver.

stockpile—Stored supplies.

surrender—To give up.

wounded—Hurt or injured, as in battle.

Learn More

Books

Crewe, Sabrina and Michael V. Uschan. *Lexington and Concord.* Milwaukee, Wisc.: Gareth Stevens, 2003.

Fradin, Dennis Brindell. *Let It Begin Here! Lexington & Concord: First Battles of the American Revolution.* New York: Walker Books, 2005.

Ingram, Scott. *Paul Revere.* San Diego: Blackbirch Press, 2004.

Kimmel, Heidi. *The Battles of Lexington and Concord.* Danbury, Conn.: Scholastic Library Publishing, 2006.

Raatma, Lucia. *The Minutemen.* Minneapolis, Minn.: Compass Point Books, 2005.

Uschan, Michael V. *Lexington and Concord.* Milwaukee, Wisc.: World Almanac Library, 2004.

Waldman, Scott P. *The Battle of Lexington and Concord.* New York: PowerKids Press, 2003.

Internet Addresses

Kidport Reference Library—Battle of Lexington and Concord

<http://www.kidport.com/RefLib/USAHistory/American Revolution/LexingtonBattle.htm>

This Web site has all the information you need on Lexington and Concord. It also has links to other battles of the American Revolution.

The Paul Revere House

<http://www.paulreverehouse.org>

Visit this Web site to see the actual house where Paul Revere lived. Do not miss the link to a page about his famous midnight ride! You will take a tour of the actual route.

INDEX